Introduction

"To everything there is a season,
and a time to every purpose
under heaven . . . "

(Ecclesiastes 3:1)

Why "Wombourne What Was"? You may well ask, when it could just as well have been "Wombourne Remembered" or perhaps "Wombourne Yesterday". I discovered that choosing a title for this small collection of old photographs was almost as hard as getting the facts right! While talking it over with Ned Williams, I thought of the Pow-Wow, and I don't mean the Indian variety. In this case it stood for "People of Wombourne — Welding our Workers" and was the grand title of a little light-hearted news-sheet issued in 1943 and 44 to Civil Defence club members, the ladies and gentlemen who were the founder members of the present Wombourne Club in Mill Lane. Each month it contained an amusing article in local dialect written by the president James Aston which he called "*Wombourne Wot Was*", and *he* knew what he was talking about.

Jim was born in Wombourne in 1886 into a family who had kept the old New Inn in School Road, and later the old Waggon and Horses (or "Brick Bridge", whichever you prefer) and was therefore well placed to get inside knowledge of the goings on of the little village of his youth. He left it for a long career in the police force and when he retired, came back to live in Sytch Lane. His articles awoke memories and brought many a laugh, and because my parents were his contempories they could often add a bit to the stories, which pleased me no end!

I can't emulate Jim's style — he was a master at it — but with respect for him and Wombourne characters from the past (and there are some in the present I'm glad to say), I have borrowed his friendly title. I hope, therefore, that the pictures will bring happy memories to you who know the village well, and be a help to anyone who wants to know it better.

But first I need to set the scene. Wombourne is a large village in the district of South Staffordshire, lying in the valley of the River Smestow of which its own Wom Brook is a tributary. It is sheltered on the east side by the Sedgley-Dudley limestone ridge and on the north by the sandstone of Orton Hills; its "mountains" on the far western horizon are the Clee Hills in Shropshire. Adjacent parishes are Himley, Swindon, Trysull, Lower Penn and Upper Penn, and the nearest towns are Wolverhampton, five miles to the north, Stourbridge, five miles to the south, and Dudley, four miles eastwards. Wombourne sits comfortably on an awful lot of sand — you only need to dig a few feet practically anywhere in the parish to reach it — and this has greatly influenced its history in the nineteenth and twentieth centuries. It was mined for industry and building, and the light soil still on top of the rest of it, is admirable for horticulture and agriculture (providing it doesn't get too thirsty). Even before 1800, the village was well known for providing good market garden produce for the nearby towns.

The first people to call this bit of England "home" said they lived by the "winding stream" and the description in their Old English words make up the name "Wombourne". Their descendants became part of the Seisdon Hundred in the

Kingdom of Mercia. By the time the Normans got to Wombourne in 1086 with their long list of questions for King William I's great land survey, it was a thriving community of 80—100 souls with a church, and *two* water mills.

In later Norman times the King and his favourites hunted across the village fields and nobody dared complain about all the damage they did, for by then Wombourne was within the Royal Forest of Kinver, which covered thousands of acres of heath and woodland, including the land attached to all the settlements therein. And woe betide any of the inhabitants caught poaching or cutting timber without permission, but I don't suppose the King had it all his own way!

The village population grew slowly through the succeeding years and didn't accelerate until the late eighteenth century. There was a slight bulge in the mid nineteenth century when the onset of the hand-made nail trade brought in new families, but it reduced when the trade died in the 1880's. The village dozed off again, that is, until the 1950's. It was then that housing needs of nearby towns, following the Second World War, hit the parish. The next thirty years brought about extensive growth in housing and industry taking the population from 3000 to 14000. There were plenty of teething troubles, and numerous shocks, but with the good will and fellowship of the people — in churches, schools, parish and district councils, all sorts of organisations, shops, factories, pubs and clubs, in fact anywhere people talk and work together — old village values have been clung to, and in a lot of ways, enhanced.

When I realised that the Wombourne of my childhood was changing, I began researching its history, and collecting photographs, documents and personal papers. Having been blessed with a mother who hardly ever threw anything away, I had a head start, and many of these ninety pictures were waiting for me at home! I apologise for the quality of some; unfortunately the poorest ones happen to be especially precious as they are all I have of certain scenes. I am well aware that not everyone wishes to be reminded of the past, and that memories come in many colours and are not always pretty. Still, a backward glance now and then should help us understand and deal better with the present, and shouldn't hurt too much, and, whether we like it or not, what happened yesterday is already history. Unfortunately, my today's are becoming yesterday and my tomorrow's today, much faster than when I was a child playing in the Wom Brook or sitting on the canal bridge watching the boats go by. Enough said.

But everyone likes a story, young and old, and even in "ordinary" Wombourne there is one at every turn, in every field and road name, and in the message at every church bell chime. I have a lot of pleasure searching them out, and if only one of the old pictures gives you some of it, then my journey is worthwhile.

From "Wombourne what is", I humbly offer you "Wombourne What Was", with my love,

May Rose Griffiths

Postscript

To 'E', or not to 'E' — that has often been the question in Wombourne. I had not thought it was necessary to comment on this local dilemma until I spotted the advertisement on the inside of the back cover concerning the book, "The Railway to Wombourn". I imagined the reader thinking we had made a mistake.

It is the little brook that flows along the floor of the valley that is at the bottom of this controversy. The Old English word that forms the second syllable of the village's name has been spelt in various ways over the years: 'bourne', 'borne', and 'burne', and sometimes in any of those versions without the final 'e'. I have checked over nine hundred references to Wombourne, in a great variety of documents dating from 1086 to 1800, and have found that it is usually the 'u' or second 'o' that is often left out, but the 'e' is generally in place.

I am sure the ordinary villager lost no sleep over it; after all, it sounded the same, and since most could not read or write, let alone spell, they were content to let the various scribes please themselves.

In the nineteenth and twentieth centuries the church and parish recorders, newsmen and map makers and others have had a go at Wombourne with the 'e' and without it, except the General Post Office which has stuck to 'Wombourne' for all mails and telephones from the beginning. The Great Western Railway Company showed some concern about it and then opted for 'Wombourn', hence the spelling used in the title of the book about the railway. The majority of the inhabitants kept to the postmark spelling. In the 1960's after some comments by newcomers to the village, the parish and district councils decided the spelling was to be 'Wombourne' and that was the end of the matter. But just afterwards along came the Ministry of Transport with their large road signs which pointed to an 'e-less' village, but even they couldn't make up their minds and the small signs pointed to 'Wombourn*e*'!

As for me, well I think it looks naked without it, and rounded and friendly with it. Mind you, the Domesday Book clerk wrote 'W*a*mburne' but everyone else fancied an 'o' there. And so, as my Dad would say when he thought it was time to end an argument — "Enough said!"

Acknowledgements

My sincere thanks to:

John and Poppy Holloway of Wombourne and Frank Blackwell of Dorchester, Oxon, for kindnesses over many years — Frank, for turning my indifferent pictures into excellent prints and slides; John for new and old photographs and sound advice; Poppy for "fetching and carrying" and pleasantly bullying me into "putting something on paper",

To the staff of record offices and libraries at Stafford, Lichfield, Wolverhampton and Wombourne for their knowledge and patience,

To everyone who has given me pictures or loaned me some for copying, for their trust and interest,

To David Cave of Swindon, Staffs, for coming to my rescue in one of my many emergencies,

To John and Carolyn Phillips of the Wombourne Wodehouse for encouragement and assistance willingly given,

To my old friends from W.E.A. days — Dr. Marie Rowlands of Birmingham and Tom Bennett of Coseley, who are always ready to share their wide knowledge and common sense with amateurs like me,

To Ned Williams, who published this, and taught me that there is more to putting a book together than sewing up the pages! And to his colleagues, for coping with the material I offered them.

To my dear friends young and old in and around Wombourne for smiling on this happy, Local History "nut", in spite of her eccentricities!

I have great need of all of you and your loving support,

Thank you.

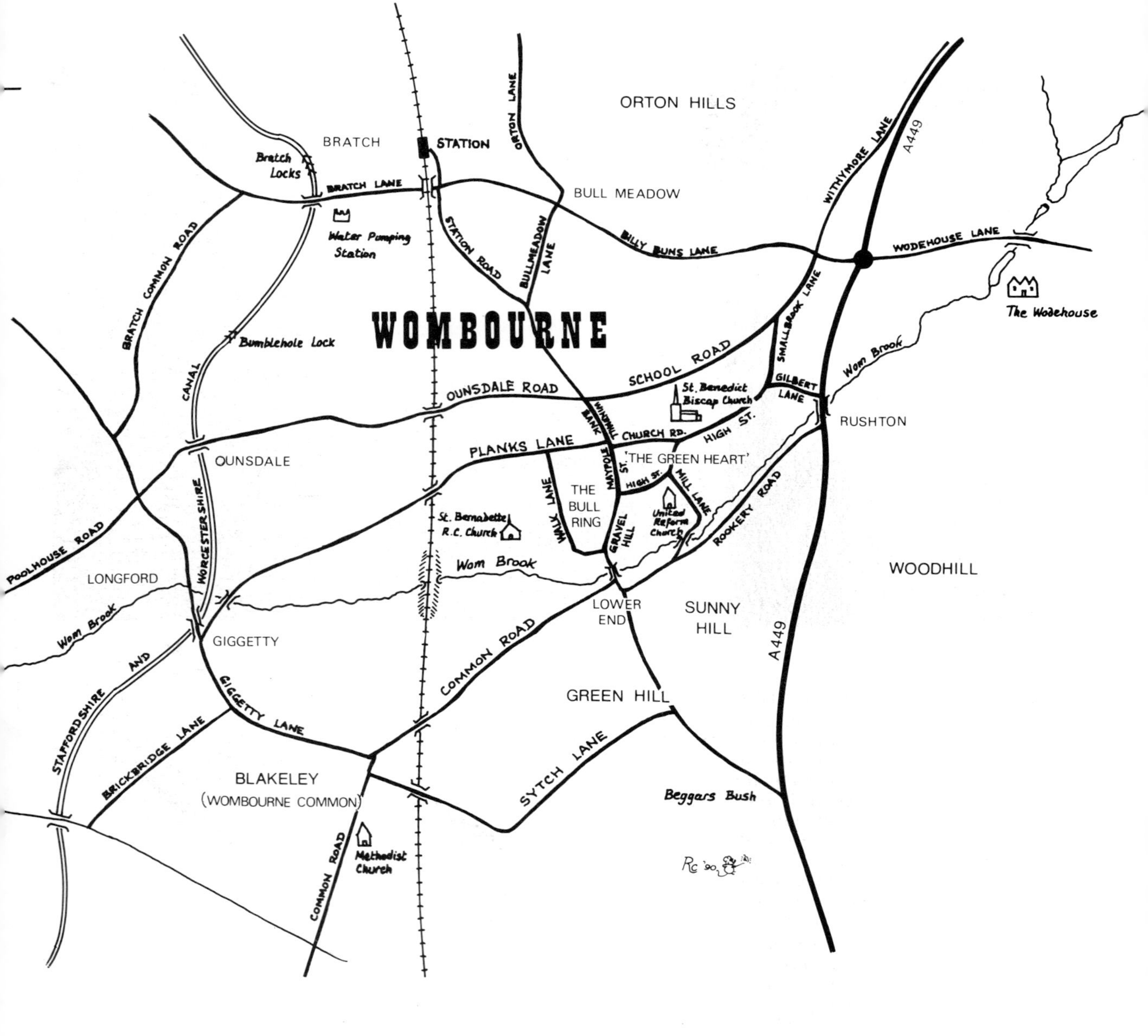
WOMBOURNE
ORTON HILLS
BRATCH
STATION
ORTON LANE
Bratch Locks
BRATCH LANE
BULL MEADOW
Water Pumping Station
STATION ROAD
BULLMEADOW LANE
BILLY BUNS LANE
WITHYMORE LANE
A449
WODEHOUSE LANE
The Wodehouse
BRATCH COMMON ROAD
Bumblehole Lock
CANAL
SMALLBROOK LANE
SCHOOL ROAD
Wom Brook
OUNSDALE ROAD
St. Benedict Biscop Church
GILBERT LANE
RUSHTON
BANK
CHURCH RD.
HIGH ST.
PLANKS LANE
'THE GREEN HEART'
OUNSDALE
MAYPOLE ST.
HIGH ST.
MILL LANE
WALK LANE
THE BULL RING
St. Bernadette R.C. Church
GRAVEL HILL
United Reform Church
ROOKERY ROAD
WORCESTERSHIRE
POOLHOUSE ROAD
LONGFORD
Wom Brook
WOODHILL
LOWER END
SUNNY HILL
Wom Brook
GIGGETTY
COMMON ROAD
A449
STAFFORDSHIRE AND
GREEN HILL
GIGGETTY LANE
BRICKBRIDGE LANE
SYTCH LANE
BLAKELEY
(WOMBOURNE COMMON)
Beggars Bush
COMMON ROAD
Methodist Church
RC '90

No. 1 Saint Benedict Biscop Church, 1900

It is certain that Wombourne had a church by 1086, thought to have been founded at the beginning of the tenth century. About 1150 Guy de Ophini, lord of the manor granted it to the Cluniac Priory of St. James at Dudley, a cell of Wenlock Abbey. It was rebuilt, but experts disagree as to how soon after, one has said thirteenth century and another fourteenth century. The most ancient parts are the local pink sandstone tower, north west corner and part of the north wall. The lovely spire of grey Hollington stone was added a century later.

In 1840 the little mediaeval building was enlarged at the east end, and north and south transepts added. Twenty six years later another 'enlargement and restoration' took place under the direction of architect George Edmund Street, when most of the nave and all the chancel were taken down, and rebuilt in the present form. By 1900 the walls and some of the roof were covered with virginia creeper, still there in the 1950's and its bright red leaves made many a passer-by stand and stare. But the new vicar was averse to its charms and had it removed.

A. Howells, Stationer

No. 2 Saint Benedict Biscop Church interior, c1909

The church is dedicated to Benedict, (a seventh century Northumbrian bishop and builder of the monasteries at Jarrow and Monkwearmouth), and as such is unique as there is no other ancient parish church with this patron saint. In the thirty years following the enlargement of 1866/7 it was furnished with a Lady Chapel, organ, font, heating system, wrought iron gates and screen to the chancel, pulpit moved from the north to south side, several pictures and statues. The Chantry memorial to Richard Bayley Marsh of Lloyd House was re-erected on the north wall.

And all those lamps — I've often thought about the person who had the job of filling them regularly with oil, trimming the wicks and polishing the brass! The pews were new in 1814 (before that there were the box type,) and most of the congregation had to pay to sit in them. Each was numbered and allocated by a special committee and woe betide anyone who sat in someone else's spot. My grandfather Fred said he did it just to see what would happen — but then he would, wouldn't he! The numbers and 'Free' — for those unable to pay — are still visible on the pew ends.

Walker's Series

No. 3 The Vicarage c1880

The ancient timber framed vicarage was near the east end of the church; the one in the picture was built in 1835 on the high ground behind. The large garden stretched from School Road to High Street. In the 1950's the present modern house was built in a corner of it. The rest was built in the 1980's, thus bringing 'Manor Gardens' and 'Vicarage Close' on to the map.

The Rev. William James Heale was 38 when he came to Wombourne in 1849, and when he died in 1897, aged 87, the villagers were desolate, after all many of them had known no other parson and he did so much for them and Wombourne. There were new schools, church restoration, Blakeley Mission built, Swindon and Trysull became separate from Wombourne (he gave £1000 for a vicarage at Trysull and was generous and helpful towards Swindon's church and vicarage) and many more good works — he even settled the debt of £2000 still to be paid on the vicarage in Wombourne. The lady in the picture is his niece Miss Gamlen who looked after him in his latter years.

The handsome eagle lectern in St. Benedict's church was given by his parishioners in his memory.

Glenda Knights

No. 4 The day they unveiled the war memorial (1920)

It was April 25th, 1920. The villagers have gathered and are waiting for the service to begin, waiting for the flag to fall away from the new memorial so that they can read — as if they didn't know them off by heart — the thirty eight names carved deep into the granite. At the front were the families of the men who would not come back to Wombourne. They stand still as the photographer takes his picture, for them to buy later in the village shop.

The little girl clutching her mother's hand (on the right) will remember this day all her life, just as she will treasure a faded letter to her mother from France, with a post script especially for her . . . "Be a good girl for Daddy . . . "

It was 'the war to end all wars', everybody said, and never in their wildest nightmares did any of them dream, that in a little over thirty years, someone would have to carve another eighteen names on their memorial . . . from another terrible war.

No. 5 The village bus stop

In the early days of motor bus transport, the Arbour Tree by the church was the terminus, and even later when one or two buses went on to Wombourne Common and Swindon for workmen or on market days, the majority went no further than the village centre. It wasn't until after the 1950's that major alterations to the service were made.

Those first vehicles were a god-send but brought their problems, and it was left to the nine parish councillors to agitate for better things. In 1913 the clerk wrote on their behalf to the bus owners that, "the extra traffic through the village was wearing out the roads, and the bus company should pay for the repairs." There were patches of oil at the bus stop and often, "a twenty seater was sent for thirty six people". The man who lived in Arbour Tree House sent a cross letter to the council saying that, "Every morning he was being disturbed because the bus driver insisted on leaving his engine running while waiting!"

The Wolverhampton to Stourbridge bus in 1915 also carried parcels, so the council built a hut near Gilbert Lane and employed a boy to put them on and off the bus and deliver the local ones.

John Holloway

No. 6 Arbour Tree House, the bus and the old tree, c1923

This fine dwelling opposite St. Benedict Biscop church may once have been three small ones; it was certainly two in 1800 when the right hand portion was the Old Bush public house kept by John Noake. In 1841 the property was recorded as 'void', but soon after was altered into a 'gentleman's residence.' (Read more about the bus under picture No. 5.)

The Arbour tree was an ancient elm. It was reported 'dangerous' in 1911, but wasn't replaced until 1925 after 'persons unknown' forced the issue by setting fire to it! The new one died almost immediately, to the consternation of the parish councillors who had made a ceremony out of its planting — even had the chairman's initials carved into the churchyard wall. Nothing daunted, they planted another. By the 1950's the middle of a road in Wombourne was no place for a tree and by then it had been hit by several vehicles. The present Arbour Tree is a sturdy young oak in the path by the club entrance opposite the church gate — long may it be part of Wombourne.

Derek Aldridge

No. 7 Ye olde Tree c1909

There are several pictures of this ancient tree which took so long a-dying. Many villagers objected to its removal even though it looked awful. It had been there as long as any of them could remember and its end would seem like theirs. Through the centuries folk had met on the spot marked by the tree to hear the 'latest' news when few of them could read or write. Their priest summoned them with the church bell and told the little crowd of a battle won or lost, a new king perhaps, yet another tax . . .

In 1895 when the parish council was formed, notices of meetings were pinned to the tree — old it may have been but still useful. Those were days when vehicles going round the village went as fast as man or horse could make them (that's Mr. Oaks in the picture), and when a curious little girl could stand safely in the middle of the road for ages, just watching a man with a camera.

Piper Series

No. 8 The Manor House

It was opposite the parish church gate and has been replaced by the modern clubhouse in the late 1960's. It should never have been pulled down; the Cricket, Tennis and Bowls Club wanted it for their headquarters, but they were over-ruled by the official planning authorities. Shame! In 1851 it is on the census return as 'Orchard House', by the twentieth century everyone knew it as the 'Manor House', and there has probably been a dwelling on the site as long as there has been a Wombourne. The previous one was 'Moisies Hall', recorded as being the 'old' hall in the seventeenth century. Several generations of the wealthy Marsh family lived here until they built Lloyd House in the 1770's.

J. Edward Chubb was its last tenant. He was good company and told many tales of his journeys for his family's lock making firm with great humour. He loved his village cricket and would watch from a little wooden chalet near the garden wall. He was a sport too — if anyone knocked a six which broke his greenhouse roof, he presented them with a bottle of whiskey!

Lloyd Sale Catalogue

No. 9 The Wombourne Institute 1990

This building in 1990 houses the Volunteer Bureau, (the 'Hand in Hand') Day Care centre, Parish office and other worthwhile groups — a little place where a lot is done. It was built in 1833 at the expense of Mrs. Sarah Dalton of Lloyd House as a day school, and replaced the Sunday school in Mr. Aston's rooms which began in 1806. My grandfather Fred Critchley attended the above school in 1856, but had to leave at the age of eight to start work!

After a new school was built in 1863, this one became the 'Wombourne Institute' and meeting place of the Mutual Improvement Society led by the vicar, and there were lectures, debates, concerts and a small library. By the early twentieth century it was better known as the 'Mens' Institute' and had acquired a billiard table. In the 1930's it was Wombourne's first clinic. The Timms bequest in the 1970's enabled the trustees to enlarge and improve, and the old motto repainted on the blank window aptly describes their aims . . . "Let's go hand in hand together, not one before another."

John Holloway

No. 10 The Parish Council Garden School, 1904

The Garden school was on land next to the Wombourne Institute in Church Road (now Telephone Exchange) run under County Council rules and with its financial help, — "37/6d for digging the ground, paying for manure, pea and bean sticks, and painting the shed". Although the clerk noted that, "work went well until footballing started nearby", the project prospered with about twelve lads. They paid 2/6d each for ground rent and the gardens were inspected three times a year, with two prizes for the best plots. In 1905 ages ranged from 13 to 16 years and the pupils were already working with regular jobs which included carting, farm labourers, carpenters and one pupil teacher. The two winners that year were Harry Blewitt, aged 14, and Edward Rogers, aged 15, both under-gardeners dreaming no doubt of being head gardeners one day.

In 1909 The Education Department at Stafford altered the school conditions and it became impracticable for it to go on, so sadly, a good venture came to an end.

Glenda Knights

No. 11 From the cricket field to the church, c1910

Col. T. B. Shaw Hellier acquired land and property in the village centre at the Lloyd Estate Sale in 1901, described in the catalogue as "the heart of Wombourne". He rented ground to the cricket club who subsequently laid it out and managed it. The lime trees around the edge were planted soon after, and now every July their honey-sweet flowers scent the air, a pleasure for all who walk that way.

In the picture — left to right, the end of 'The Fold' houses (picture 13) two others lie back and only the roof apex is visible (in 1990's 'Eric's shop' and offices); Carrier's shed (see picture No. 12) and more houses to Love Alley; the Wombourne Institute and the Manor House stables — the house itself is on the far right.

The ancient name for this "heart of Wombourne" is Dovecote Close. Before 1800 there was a horse pond in the corner near the stables.

David Ball

No. 12 Church Street c1956

It is 'Church *Road*' in 1990, but until 1938 it was 'Over Street'. On the left of the picture is the end of 'The Fold' — see No. 13. The building farther along with the corrugated tin roof was Carrier's workshop, near to the home of this family of many talents and pursuits — carpenters, house builders, shop keepers, bell ringers, cricketers, pigeon fanciers 'etcetera', and village undertakers as well. It was the coffin making bit that overawed us children who peeped into the shed on the way to school, in the hope we might see "something", but ready to run if we did! When the site was redeveloped it was rightly named 'Carriers Fold'.

Notice the wall — in the days of the picture pedestrians could not enjoy walking under the lovely lime trees, for they were then within the sports ground perimeter. I like it better now that the 'green heart' is in full view of passers by, although there are still people in the village who would have preferred the wall left as it was — and I respect their opinions.

Crowe's Series

No. 13 The Fold, Church Road, c1950

"The Fold" was the name of an "L" shaped group of almshouses built between 1820 and 1840 on land formerly known as "Pound Close". Since both "fold" and "pound" are to do with animals it is easy to see how the name changed. Originally it had been an enclosed field where strayed animals were put until claimed, and the fine paid by the owner if he wanted his wandering creatures back.

It is now the site of the Community centre. In the picture there is a noticeboard on which were the plans for the new hall. For some years before the Second World War a hard working committee had raised funds for such a project. When eventually the time for building came around, they only had 3/13 of the money needed — costs had escalated after the war — and so it was that the County Council stepped in with the rest. Afterwards some of the back land was used for a library.

George Howell

No. 14 Windmill Bank 1933

These houses were at the bottom of Windmill Bank, photographed looking eastwards from the top of Planks Lane. A view from the same place in the late twentieth century would show landscaped gardens, library and Community Centre. A lot of people had their homes "up the Bank", a close knit community in little houses most of which were built before 1800 — also see the next two pictures.

On the 1841 Tithe map, the whole stretch of road from the top of the Bank, including present Maypole Street and Gravel Hill, was shown as "Windmill Bank Street." It was much later that the middle bit became "Maypole Street" named after an ancient pub called "The Maypole" — "Wombourne Farm" was built on its site and that is now a shop called "The Gallery" and offices. "Gravel Hill" was probably a reference to its state before or after the repair needed on the slope after bad storms. Old Wombourne it seems was content with Windmill Bank Street for the lot!

Chris Perkins

No. 15 Windmill Bank 1935

The British Legion striding down the Bank in the church parade during George V Jubilee celebrations. This picture gives a good view of the street as it was until demolition started a few years later. It was taken from the top of Planks Lane and there were several more houses between there and the junction with Church Road (where the toilets and gardens are now) and on the opposite side, now the site of the shops.

There was a large detached house on the Bank corner of Planks Lane which was the home of the village constable in the 1930's — the "lock-up" was a little brick building without windows in the garden, and unfortunately I wasn't quick enough to get its picture before the shop-builders moved in. I don't suppose those who occupied it were worried about remembering how it looked!

Don Henty

No. 16 Windmill Bank 1920's

Looking down the Bank, as it was until the late 1930's. Long before then, perhaps as much as five centuries, it was the way to a windmill on the piece of ground where the present New Inn now stands. I think they should have called that pub "The Windmill", a bit more imaginative than being just "New" — maybe someone will have it altered one day; who knows? The earliest record of a windmill in Wombourne is 1358 and it could well have been there. There was one off Common Road in 1600 and the last was on present Waverley Gardens land in the nineteenth century, but the one which gave its name to the little hill had gone long before 1800.

The Bank is a bit steep with its modern tarmac, just imagine what it was like when it was rough and pitted with cart ruts and John Wombourne had to get his yearly grain harvest up to the mill — and even trickier going down! Imagine too, the glorious sight of the big brown sails turning as they caught the west wind from over the Clee Hills . . . in another time and other ways of doing things.

William Sadler

No. 17 The old New Inn, School Road, c1923

"Potter" Day and his son outside their pub — Houses Nos. 14, 16 now on the site.

Inns have played many roles over and above their primary function all through the ages — meeting places for guilds and societies, auctions, coroner's inquests and courts, post office, doctor's surgery, council meetings and so on. At the New Inn for example . . . "On Thursday January 31, 1811, at 3 o'clock in the afternoon precisely at Mr. Aston's, the New Inn, 100 capital ash trees for sale, 84 elm, 14 alder, 5 birch and 1 walnut, growing on lands at the Lloyd and Wombourne . . . " Another occasion was the "Annual show for gooseberries and carnations will be held on Aug. 2nd. 1813 . . . " and there were many more such days.

Mr. Aston also let his rooms for a Sunday school in 1806 until 1833 (see more under picture No. 9) where the children were taught to read and write as well as get religious instruction — after all they had no time in the week for such a luxury since most of them were already at work as long as there was daylight.

No. 18 School Lane c1900

In the seventeenth century this was recorded as "the way to Bobbington", and by 1808 it was "Womborne Lane". After a new vicarage was built in 1835 it became "Vicarage Lane" and, likewise, after the new school was built in 1863 it changed to "School Lane". In the 1930's it was a "*road*"!

The land behind the big elms on the right was given to the parish for the churchyard extension in 1901, and until needed in the 1950's was a public recreation ground ("The Rec"), and an extra school playground. Along the edge were stout iron posts with loops of thick spiky chains between, certainly not intended for swinging on, but with a bit of care and a few wriggles any child could manage it without permanent injury — when teacher wasn't looking!

At near right of the picture is the corner of the old New Inn and next to it is Jasmine Villa. At one time the field opposite was the venue of travelling fairs; you could hear the music at Wombourne Common but few complained — after all fair days were very special, and made many a memory for villagers of all ages.

Donald Linney

No. 19 St. Benedict Biscop School, c1960

In 1863, the new National School, with headmasters' house attached, was Wombourne's pride, and it served us well for a century. Modern box-like constructions may be easier on maintenance and heating, but they often lack character and age doesn't seem to give them dignity. I hope this picture will give pleasure to old pupils, and even if they had the cane there occasionally, I'm sure the pain of it was forgotten long ago.

In the early days boys and girls were separated in classroom and playground. An emergency like a stove being out of order or one part being decorated would cause them to be put together and this was duly noted in the log book. I can almost hear the headmaster's sigh of relief when things got back to normal.

Two precious bits of the old days have survived — the iron cross as strong and meaningful as always, is now on the wall by the front entrance of the present building, and the bell as clear as ever, is in the foyer. Together they serve as a link between old and new.

John Holloway

No. 20 The staff of the village school, c1880

John Wormington was headmaster from 1876 to 1904. His biggest problem was not in teaching the children, but getting them to come to school! Bye laws said they should attend ten times a week, that is, each morning and afternoon, but few did. Threats and fines to parents made no difference, if the children could earn pennies working in fields and gardens, then why not? There were plenty of other distractions, local wakes, club walks, chapel and church tea parties were always on weekdays, to say nothing of such excitement as "the day they cleaned out the mill pool" — more fun than lessons. In 1877 gales brought down so many trees children were employed picking up the branches. When Mr. Gladstone visited the village in 1888, so few attended, the school was closed.

More seriously, and sadly annually, the school was closed for weeks because of epidemics like measles, whooping cough and scarlet fever, when several pupils died; and when there were "severe weather conditions", "roads unfit to be on", "school cold and dark". Once the headmaster noted in his log book "today the ink froze in the ink wells . . . " Oh my!

No. 21 Wombourne schoolchildren 1895

A smart new school was built for Wombourne's children in 1863 and here are a few of them some twenty two years later, keeping still for the photographer. Girls in their white "pinnies", boys with jackets buttoned up to the neck, all with stout boots — they needed them on those lanes! Elizabeth Critchley on the left, was my mother's aunt, and very handy with the cane. She walloped her nephews and nieces more than the others, mother said, just to prove she had no favourites! By the time I met her she was a dignified kind old lady with no cane.

At this time there were 160 pupils on the register, and Mr. Wormington the headmaster had a testimonial from the Bishop of Lichfield for their high attainments in religious knowledge.

These were the lads who would be fighting for Wombourne and England in eighteen years time, and these are the girls who would be waiting for them to come back . . . but in 1895 their biggest worry was my Aunt Liz!

No. 22 A war-time cookery class

Florence Apse, wife of headmaster John Apse, with her cookery class on 9 November 1917, and some of the fruit they had been bottling. I'll have to guess at what was in the bowls, but seeing the date I reckon it was Christmas puddings.

These young ladies, all aged about thirteen were already capable of cooking for a family. Not for them shop shelves stacked with "convenience foods", and everything in or out of season in tins or frozen packs. They knew the proper way of making any dish, and if they could have been told that their grandchildren would buy a packet of mystery, add water to it and just heat it, or buy tins of ready made rice pudding and custard for the dinner table, they would wonder what sort of world would follow theirs. The meals they learned to make without fancy saucepans and cookers were as good as any today, and there are many folks who would say, better. Mrs. Apse was a founder member of the Womens Institute in Wombourne and its treasurer for 28 years, an excellent cook and housewife — so the headmaster was well looked after.

No. 23 Wombourne School Choir 1925

Every single one of them has the look of the cat who got the cream. They had just won three first prizes at a festival and the "Gaffer" and Miss Lewis were proud of them!

John Apse was headmaster of the village school from 1906 to 1946. He was far-sighted in his attitude to education, and in other things — he had one of the first cars in Wombourne! He loved God and all life, and did his utmost to transmit his values and ideals to his staff and pupils. "Johnny" — another of his nicknames — was a strict disciplinarian and one word or glance from him was enough to quieten any situation — but he tempered it with humour and tolerance. Apart from the usual lessons the children had singing and dancing, gardening and poultry and beekeeping and took part in every function the village year had to offer. His former pupils forgot how many times he had to give them the cane and in respect called him "sir" even when they were parents themselves and he was an old man. And what is more they named "Apse Close" after him, and the north gate of the churchyard (now about where this picture was taken) is the "Apse Gate".

No. 24 The School Outing (1) 1932

In the 1920's and 30's, on the second Saturday in July, John Apse, village schoolmaster, Pied Piper for a day, spirited away all the children and most of their families to such far away magic places as Bournemouth, Torquay, Brighton and the lovely Welsh coast. The few who stayed behind said they couldn't settle to do anything in the deserted village, but just wait for the day to pass. "Johnny" hired a fourteen coach train, (the middle one was used as a bar) which left the Bratch and Himley just after dawn on what was always a perfect morning. The money for this adventure was collected each week at school and if a child hadn't enough by July, Johnny always found the rest for them.

And what a day they had. Some had smart bathing suits (see next picture), others just paddled and lazed on the sands. It didn't matter how much of your knickers you showed — they had probably been bought new for the occasion anyway — because who cared! There was no point in going at all if you didn't put your feet at least into the briny. At home there was only the Wom Brook!

No. 25 The Annual Outing (2) Seaside here we come!

Kath Bullock, Fern Spark, John Butcher, Rosie Caddick and Hilda Holder having a whale of a time! Wearing the latest in 1930's swimwear they managed to pack as much fun into a day as some others might do in a fortnight now, and what is more, the memory of it has lasted to give them many a laugh in the years which have followed.

How their Pied Piper got them back to Wombourne in good order is a puzzle — there were a few who were left behind asleep on the beech or dallying in a pub — but apart from suchlike he managed it well. He made sure there was enough stock in the bar for the journey home and it is a miracle the train kept on the line with the hilarity produced. Eventually when it ran dry, the singers were hoarse, the exhausted children had given up running up and down the corridors and the lovers had found each other, all was quiet until they had to fall out of the train at the Bratch — 24 hours after they had left it. No cars to get them home, just a long walk, but even that didn't spoil their glorious day's outing.

No. 26 Waverley House 1901

This ancient farm house was demolished in the 1960's, and the present police station built on the site in 1971. In 1820 it was the home and premises of William Hayward, late of Trysull; a farmer and butcher. In the twentieth century it was divided into two dwellings. Waverley House was a fine building and ought to have been preserved. Thankfully the name was not lost and it lives on in "Waverley Gardens" about a hundred yards away (as any respectable crow might fly); a cul de sac off School Road.

The picture shows the Small Brook running at the side of the road — now inside a pipe — and although very small indeed as brooks go, managed to cause trouble after heavy rain. The two houses on the right of the picture — one was a shop — lay against Arbour Tree House garden wall, and the occupants had to suffer that Small Brook in their front rooms sometimes as well as on their doorsteps.

Lloyd Sale Catalogue

No. 27 The Vine Inn, High Street, before 1900

Were they going in or coming out?

In a sale held at the New Inn in 1831 the property was described as a "neat well built freehold dwelling house, with stable, outbuildings and a large garden, late in the occupation of Mr. Jesse Cartwright, deceased, situate in the pleasant, healthful and retired village of Wombourne, near to the turnpike road from Wolverhampton to Stourbridge, . . . roomy and convenient, sheltered from the north and east winds and within three minutes walk of the church." It was still a private house in 1851, but by 1861 it was the Vine Inn.

I am reminded of a story of a pony who lived about this time at Battlefield and who took her wealthy master regularly to the Vine. When he over imbibed — which was frequently — the other customers would load him into the trap, give the pony a brief command and off she would trot, off down Gilbert Lane and up the hill home. That is an example of real horse power in conjunction with horse sense. No need for a breathalyser with a pony like that!

Glenda Knights

No. 28 The Village Hall, High Street, Opening Day 1927

The Womens' Institute movement began in Wombourne in 1920 and meetings were in Slater's hut, then at the top of Planks Lane. In 1927 Mrs. Evelyn Shaw Hellier gave land at the corner of the Townsend meadows for a hall, and here she is performing the opening ceremony. It is still owned and maintained by W.I. members.

When the school was built in 1863 it was offered for use to the village for any kind of public gathering, church, civic and social. In 1927 the new hall took on a similar role and became important not only to the W.I. movement but to all needs. In wartime especially it was invaluable — lectures for air raid precautions and emergencies, money raising for various war efforts, and meetings. Here came tired and wondering evacuees from London and Birmingham to await their new addresses; here came parcels of fruit from Australia to be distributed round the village; and here it was that the W.I. members made-do-and-mended, canned fruit and vegetables, and generally waged their own war on shortages. It was and still is a well-used building.

No. 29 Across Townsend meadows from Rushford, 1930

"The Townsend meadows" is the correct name for the fields opposite the Bush public house, and was the point at which the houses and crofts of the medieval settlement gave way to the open fields and woodland. The name was in use on deeds before 1260.

From left to right — a glimpse of Arbour Tree House, the church spire, Waverley House, the Village Hall, the Vine Inn, a shop and house on what is now car park, and on the far right the Bush pub. Originally there were two fields, divided by a hawthorn hedge which went from High Street down to the brook.

These were the meadows on which Wombourne held its "great" Floral Fete and Gymkhana in the mid twentieth century years, a lovely site for the village unforgettable annual "day out".

Crowe's Series

No. 30 Smallbrook 1968

"Smallbrook" is the most recent name for the area at the east end of present High Street where it meets Gilbert Lane and Smallbrook Lane. You could call it by its medieval name of "Townsend" or the nineteenth century one of "Sodom", whichever you fancy since all three have been official at one time or another. These houses, built before 1800, were pulled down to make way for Waterfield House (sheltered accommodation for the elderly) in the 1980's. The house just visible on the left was at right angles to the road.

As for it being "Townsend" see picture No. 29; the name was already old by 1260 when Adam de Byrnhull granted land for five shillings to William Attetounesend. The Smallbrook from Orton Hills dives down into a pipe by the willows at the road junction — it once ran open all down High Street (and that was Over Street then) — Oh, isn't it confusing!

As for the "Sodom" bit, well, *you* guess!

No. 31 Show Day (1) 1930

The Floral Fete Day was one on which everyone found something worth remembering, met old friends and made new ones, and generally had a good day out. The old poster will tell the story for me. After 1947, when a horse show and gymkhana were added, as many as 10,000 people flocked to the fields at Gilbert Lane, but I don't think the beer ever ran out and hooliganism was unheard of. Of course there was plenty of argy-bargy over who had won the prizes and who should have done, but that was all part of the fun.

Wombourne, like most local villages, had had shows of one kind and another since the early nineteenth century, like the annual Gooseberry show in the New Inn in 1813, to the great 1880 days which were forerunners of the ones advertised above. In the 1930's local bus companies fell over backwards to transport the visitors (have a look at the small print at the bottom of the poster) and there were even cheap trips on the *train*! Happy Days!

WOMBOURNE

FLORAL FETE

(Under the auspices of the Wombourne Women's Institute)

Saturday, July 26th, 1930.

OPENING CEREMONY AT 2-30 P.M. BY

LADY MANDER

Grand Display of Flowers, Fruit and Vegetables, and Women's Institute Handicrafts.

Motor Cycle Novelty Races.

GREAT

BOXING TOURNAMENT

Arranged by Col: Serg. H. Curzon. Three Contests.

10 Rds. BONNY EVANS, W'hampton v. TOM CASHMORE, Walsall
Winner of over 100 contests.
6 ,, ALF COTTRILL, ,, v. JIM REDFERN, ,,
Premier Featherweight.
6 ,, TED HUGHES, ,, v. TED PUGH, Wolverhampton.
Special 4 rounds; HARRY CURZON'S MIDGETS.

WHIPPETT HANDICAP

Prizes: £5. £1/10/0. 10/0.
Entrance Fee, 1/6 for 1st Dog, 1/0 each after.
All Dogs to be weighed on ground at 4p.m. 30 lb limit.
Entries to Mr. H. Ashby, Professional Handicapper E.N P.S.A., 18 Perry St., Darlaston, by Wednesday, 23rd July

Special attraction: Whippett versus Pigeon Race.

ATTRACTIVE SIDE SHOWS. All the Fun of the Fair.

Novel Attractions including Gee Whizz, Hoop-La, Aunt Sally, Cocoanut Shy, etc., etc.

Gornal Wood Silver Band.

DANCING after 7 o'clock.

LICENSED CATERING (BUTLERS' ALES etc,)
TEAS PROVIDED by Members of Wombourne Women's Institute in the W.I. Village Hall at 1s. each
ALSO LIGHT REFRESHMENT BUFFET.

Admission 1s. Children 6d. AFTER 7 o'clock: SIXPENCE

Wolverhampton Corporation 'Buses will run all day at frequent intervals. Special 'Bus Service from Sedgley in the Afternoon.
Extra 'Buses for Return Services. Show Ground on Wolverhampton and Stourbridge Red 'Bus Route.
Cheap Tickets, (Single fare, Double Journey G W R to Wombourne Station. Special train leaving Wombourne 9-30 p m
Schedules and further information from H Gittins, Hon Sec, Greenhill, Wombourne

FRED G. LUNT, PRINTER, WORDSLEY

No. 32 Show Day (2) 1968

Show Day like Outing Day was not to be missed. It was restarted after the Second World War in 1947 by a committee of members of the W.I., the Cricket, Tennis and Bowls club and the Civil Defence club. The latter eventually dropped out and the other two kept it going for nearly twenty years. It took a large number of men and women a year to plan, a week on the field to prepare and cost in the 1960's nearly a thousand pounds in tentage, publicity and prizes. The horticultural section occupied the large marquee (centre picture) and two others close by; the rest were bar and refreshments, first aid, sideshows, trade stands etc.

The big show ring on the left (out of the picture) was run under B.S.J.A. rules and attracted some of the best young riders in these Midland counties, especially the Foxhunter class which led a number of them to White City. It was a lot of work and a lot of fun — some years the committee had to help get the hay off the field first! Sadly, rising costs and other problems killed it. I didn't dream when I took this picture that I was recording the end of an era.

No. 33 The Wombourne Wodehouse (pronounced Woodhouse) before 1872

For about 800 years there has been a home here on the hillside above the Wom Brook on the north-eastern edge of the parish — a "house in the wood" from which the early family took its name of "Woodhouse". Today the heart of the house is a medieval timber-framed building dated 1350, and lived in as much now as at any time during the past centuries. The "Woodhouse" has never been sold, but it was mortgaged once. The occupiers have altered and added according to their particular fancy, so like Topsy it has "just growed" into the fascinating whole it is in the late twentieth century.

The picture above is the earliest photograph (dated before 1872) and shows the early nineteenth century west front, the roofline of tall chimneys, the Flemish gables and sash windows. It was remodelled in 1872/3 and then at the end of the century two of the five gables were replaced by a parapet with the motto "Domum Dulce Domum" — Home Sweet Home — instead of balusters. Compare this picture with No. 34.

John Phillips

No. 34 The Wombourne Wodehouse (2) 1990

The folk who lived here first and took Woodhouse for their name in the late thirteenth century, held the property until the early eighteenth century, from whom it passed to the Helliers, the Shaw Helliers and to John and Carolyn Phillips in 1981. It is not just a charming house set in pleasant gardens, it is primarily a welcoming home, which the owners share happily with visitors at a variety of functions, and thus benefit innumerable charities and causes, local and national.

There are terraced lawns which drop down to the mere, all kinds of flowers and shrubs, quiet paths which wind through the wood along the brookside . . . and many lovely trees. It is a "come back again place" and I offer you a verse which is on another Staffordshire house, and hope to be forgiven for borrowing it for the "Woodhouse".

Traveller if you pass this way
A blessing on this house I pray,
And if you've time — I beg your pardon —
Spare another for the garden.

(Read the Victoria County History, Vol. XX 1984, pages 204-6 for much more about "the house in the wood.")

John Holloway

No. 35 The Harvest gate in the Wodehouse garden

This lovely old gate made of harvest implements epitomises for me what my village was for more than a thousand years, and to some extent still is. For in spite of extensive residential and industrial development since the 1950's, its three and a half thousand acres are largely agricultural. At the moment it has the best of two worlds, in one are the amenities and benefits brought about by and for its enlarged community, and in the other the delights of the natural life of the fields, woods and hedgerows all around it — the precious green circle its inhabitants will fight to keep intact.

The tools in the gate were for a slower Wombourne. The sound of the rhythmic swish, swish, of a dozen men with scythes cutting a field of ripe grain has gone from our countryside, and one man and a great machine can do in a day in harvest time what was once a week's work for the whole village. But there is no harm in looking back occasionally at times past, especially if the nostalgia brings into mind some place and some one worth remembering . . .

John Holloway

No. 36 "An early cricket team" c1870 or "In the beginning!"

Unfortunately I have no record of the names of these gentlemen but I am glad to have their picture. They deserve to go into posterity, not only for their attire (especially hats) but for the dignity of their bearing. They would have taken on Australia, given the chance, let alone a neighbouring village! I am sure they did both the game and Wombourne credit.

I expect they had a fund of stories worth relating as well, and I am reminded of one my father told of another local team in the late nineteenth century — about the same time as the above picture. The game was a slow one, the afternoon was very hot, and the umpire called "Out!" to a young batsman who argued that he was *not*. The umpire's decision was final and as the young man walked away he shouted "I was *not* out, and *you know* I wasn't!" to which the reply came "All right, you were not out, but you've been in long enough!"

Glenda Knights

No. 37 Wombourne Cricket Field 1910

In April 1867, the Mutual Improvement Society members made plans, "to rent Mr. Haywards field at Sodom (top of Gilbert Lane) for cricket at £2. 10s. for the season, and a boy to be paid 3d a week to carry the bats to and fro." In 1874 the game was played on a field at Wodehouse corner, members paying 2d a week.

In 1901 Col. T. B. Shaw Hellier rented land in the village centre to the club (see picture No. 11), and then in 1945 Miss Molly Shaw Hellier handed it over to the County Council "to be kept always as an open space for recreation." When thanking her the chairman said, "that all people would appreciate this generous and public spirited gift and that the land would be preserved for ever in the way Miss Shaw Hellier intended."

The picture also shows the buildings of Maypole Street, the bottom of Windmill Bank, and dimly, the young lime trees against the wall.

No. 38 High Street, late 1950's

There is a glimpse of the Small Brook, a piece of the old wall and a view of the cottages, as yet unaltered. When the road widening and removal of the wall was planned (late 1950's), the villagers divided "for" and "against" losing their central landmark. There were even letters to the editor of the Express and Star, some funny and some not so funny. The following poem appeared as one of them.

(It is doubtful if it ever was "village green", but that is another story).

Though cricket matches I have seen,
I've yet to see them all,
There's one on Wombourne's village green
behind the village wall.
Ah, what controversy has raged,
"To see or not to see",
O'er village wall a war is waged
"To be or not to be",
Though fence may come and wall may yield,
one thing we must endeavour
We must retain our cricket field
and village green for ever!

Signed "*Evergreen*"

Crowe's Series

No. 39 Wombourne Congregational Church, Mill Lane, 1900

Records show that non-conformity began in Wombourne in the sixteenth century. By 1800 licences were needed from the Bishop for cottage meetings; the lists give the various locations and there were several in Wombourne. In 1835 Congregationalists began renting a barn at Lower End (see picture No. 51) into which they put a ceiling, furniture and painted the walls. Into this little space squeezed 140 adults and children.

In 1851 a proper church was built at the top of Mill Lane and in 1870 a vestry and school room added. The spire was removed during renovations in 1914. A row of cottages down the lane were demolished and in 1957 A. J. Allen of Greenhill House built a hall in memory of his wife Nan. At the same time the front door was blocked, another opened in the side and the interior plan reversed. There were more additions in the 1980's.

A few yards of a branch of the Small Brook can just be seen on the left of the picture.

No. 40 The Floodgates c1905

The little Wom Brook has worked hard for the village since Saxon days. First it gave the settlement its name and then water and power for generations. As late as 1890 it was feeding four watermills within less than two miles — at Wodehouse, Mill Lane, Lower End and Heath Mill. The pool at Mill Lane was drained about 1900 and the people in the picture are standing on a path they called "The Floodgates" but later generations preferred the name "Pool Dam".

Wombourne had two mills in 1086 and although it is hard to prove, I like to think one was the Mill Lane site. There has certainly been a mill here for centuries working as either corn or blade mill. By 1840 it was a Blade Mill only, and ended its days as the premises of a scythe manufacturer.

A. Howells Stationer

No. 41 The Rookery

In 1841 four cottages near the brook by Rushford Bridge (see picture 43) were described as being at "the Rookery" and presumably were so called because of the obvious, that is, that there was or had been a well established rookery near by. Rookery Lane was then little more than a track and the few houses at the other end of it were better known as "Lower End", the names of the roads were not as important as the "district" name. People said they lived at "The Bratch", at "Bullmeadow" or perhaps "up the Bank" and so on. There were no road signs and few houses had names, but everyone knew where everyone else lived and "addresses" as we think of them were irrelevant.

The row of nailer's houses in the picture were on the hill side of the present Rookery Lane (it has been "Road" as well) about half way between Rushford and the bottom of Battlefield Lane, now replaced by modern dwellings.

No. 42 A Railway tragedy

This picture was taken near Rushford Bridge at the end of Rookery Road. It was the funeral of a local lad killed while working on the construction of Great Western Railway's line through the parish. The cottages behind the procession were between the road and the brook, and it is hard to imagine now when looking at the site (the end of the Wombrook Walk) that four houses and nailshops could have been put in so narrow a space. I believe that they were pulled down in the early 1930's.

Hiram Carrier, man of all trades — in this case undertaker — is the tall man standing near the wall on the right. It is his family which is remembered in "Carriers Fold" off Church Road, see more under picture No. 12.

Glenda Knights

No. 43 Red Lion Hill 1930

If you told a stranger that this was Red Lion Hill, Battlefield Hill, Stourbridge Road, the A449 or Rushford, he would be confused but you would not be wrong. After all a village which is never sure how to spell its own name can be forgiven for having five names for what is the same place! Old documents can add to the list — in the Middle Ages it was "the road from Worcester to Chester"; in 1612 it was "the King's highwaye betwixt Wolverhampton and Sturbridge"; in the eighteenth century it was "the Turnpike road" (Himley and Coalway Road were the nearest toll houses); and in 1840 it appeared on a map as "Hampton Way"! The mid twentieth century named it "the Mile of Death" as there were so many accidents.

The Red Lion is Wombourne's oldest inn — note the hitching post near to the sign, if petrol keeps increasing we will need to use such things again!

At this time the village police station was the large house, seen here with a car parked outside, almost opposite the pub. The crest is just visible over the door.

Crowe's Series

No. 44 High Street until the late 1950's

This was once called Moisies Hall Street, but it has changed a bit since then. In the picture is postman Jim Wood, with the Small Brook in its little trough at his feet. On the left bit of wall can be seen a faint "Lot 94", a relic of the 1901 sale when the land of Dovecote Close was divided into lots for building. Mercifully Col. T. B. Shaw Hellier bought it and the rest is cricket club history. The opening where the other man is standing was a short road with several nailshops in 1841.

The Small Brook is now below the footpath and does not come into daylight until it drops into the Wom Brook just past Walk House. Although the wall was too high for most folk to look over and watch the sport on the other side, its crumbling state allowed for plenty of footholds. It was a simple feat to climb up and sit on the top — and even I did it!

Walkers Series

No. 45 Post Office, High Street, 1935

This was Walker's shop and Wombourne's third post office. The first was a little shop next to Ivy House in Maypole Street (the manager's office of Lloyd's Bank now occupies that site); the second is now the doctor's surgery in High Street; the fourth and present one lower down started life as a butcher's shop. In the backroom of the one pictured above was housed the first manual telephone exchange.

In the picture Lily Crowe (Mrs. Walker's daughter) and husband Frank are decorating the office for the 1935 Silver Jubilee. These premises were famous locally for more than being a post office and shop — namely Mrs. Walker's home-made ice cream. It was like none other before or since, and if ambrosia is the food of the Gods then this was ambrosia. It was thick and creamy and the villagers collected it in basins and jugs for only a few pennies. And if I tell you that I once met a man in the Isle of Skye who, when I said I came from Wombourne in Staffordshire and that he wouldn't have heard of it, answered, "I have, and I've had some of Mrs. Walker's ice cream!" There's fame for you.

George Howell

No. 46 A Nailwarehouse in the Bull Ring

The domestic hand-made nail trade developed in Wombourne in the early nineteenth century and by 1850 there were tiny cramped workshops attached to many of the cottages. Whole families worked from sunrise to sunset in hot filthy conditions for low return. Bundles of rods weighing ½ hundredweight (25 kg.) were collected from the warehouse and the finished nails returned, and things were not always fair on either side, workman or master. It was hard work and there was little time for leisure. In Wombourne records children of eight and nine are shown as "nailers" — no joy for them. By 1880 the trade had gone from the village as machine made nails were being made more cheaply in nearby towns.

The Bull Ring — the wide road junction of High Street, Gravel Hill and Maypole Street — was the place where our ancestors enjoyed the cruel sport of bull baiting. The unfortunate animal was tethered to a 25 yard long rope and then set on by dogs, a "sport" finally banned in England in 1835. The warehouse site is Barclays Bank in 1990. The scots pine in the picture has survived.

No. 47 Gravel Hill 1961

This view is from the bend of Gravel Hill, looking towards the Bull Ring and the village centre. The high wall on the left along the garden of Gravel Hill House was built with sandstone blocks removed from St. Benedict's church during alterations in 1866/7. The cottages on the right have been replaced by the gardens in front of the Civic Centre — the nearest one was the surgery of Dr. Spackman and Dr. Dukes, until a more modern one was built a bit lower down.

The house just visible on the left is dated 1768. Next to it in the late nineteenth century and early twentieth century was the home and premises of William Wellings, wheel wright and undertaker and other accomplishments. Netley House, just out of the picture, was the home of a maltster, the malt house was behind on what is now the garden of present Grove Cottage next door. But that was a long, long time ago, and the village had another malthouse after that in Walk Lane.

No. 48 The Maltings, Walk Lane

The last maltings in Wombourne. I know of two earlier sites — one behind present Netley House on Gravel Hill, and one behind the old New Inn in School Road. Here the village barley became malt for John Wombourne, who had as deep a thirst then as now, even though he doesn't get paid in ale as he did once. The church accounts have many entries like 1786 — "ale for men one shilling" and "one days work at the bells and ale 1/6". A big job in the churchyard in 1801 cost 27/6 but included in that was "beer for men for the whole time 4s. 6d.", so a sixth of the bill was for drink! No wonder we needed a big maltings! The old building in the picture had a wealth of superb timbers and wooden machinery.

The present "Maltings" is a number of flatlets for elderly people. There is at least one tie between the old and new usage of the site, as two of the lovely wooden tools, a spade and fork used when making barley into malt, are mounted on the lounge wall — and handsome they look.

John Holloway

No. 49 Green Hill and Lower End c1950

There was a green hill . . . yesterday . . .

The 300 feet (91 metre) contour line crosses the parish east-west from Baggeridge to Swindon and on the way takes in Wood Hill, Birch Hill, Sunny Hill, Green Hill, and what used to be called Soldiers Hill on the Swindon boundary.

The 1841 Tithe map shows the cottage on the corner of Gravel Hill and Rookery Road as "chapel" (see reason under picture No. 51), the one opposite was a public house. A century later the words "Cottage Spring Ales" was still visible in white paint on one wall. When it was demolished and a new house built on the land behind, the owner chose "Cottage Spring" for its name. There was a wire fence behind the wall of Sheepcote Close on the right of the hill, because the low sandstone wall was child's play for energetic cattle if they felt the need to wander.

The poplars on the horizon gave their name to "Poplar Close" when the green hill was built over.

No. 50 Walk House Farm 1901

The house still stands at the bend of Walk Lane, but the dovecotes have long since gone. It was possibly the site of the home of the wealthy Smith family, millers before the seventeenth century. In 1818 Richard Bayley Marsh of Lloyd House bought it and by 1841 it was rented by farmer John Hill — who employed 10 men on his 400 acres. He lived in this house with his wife Mary, four children, two sisters in law, a governess and five servants. In 1881 it was unoccupied — fortunes change for houses as well as people. Today it is an appealing dwelling in a lovely garden and its adjacent meadows are part of the Wombourne Walk. It is likely that the name came from the ancient rope walk nearby.

During World War II, a bomb fell fifty yards from the front of Walk House, but although the building was damaged, the brook and the lovely garden took most of the impact.

Lloyd Sale Catalogue

No. 51 Lower End c1950

"Lower End" was a cluster of eighteenth century and nineteenth century houses centred on the junction with Common Road, Green Hill and Rookery Road, long before there were such things as road signs in Wombourne. It got its name from the bridge close by — the "lower" or "nether" bridge over the brook, as distinct from the one at Rushford upstream occasionally called the "upper" bridge.

Left to right, a glimpse of the old maltings, with Sheepcote close in front; Gravel Hill House — in the 1930's the home and office of the Registrar of Births and Deaths (until 1946), behind it was the council chamber where both district and parish council met for many years until the new one was built a bit higher up the hill; Fox's butchers shop was on the bend opposite, in the picture only the barn remains. The building on the near right (with a shop-type window) was once a barn attached to the cottage. In 1835 it was renovated and furnished by a group of nonconformists and used as a chapel and school-room until they were able to build the one at the top of Mill Lane, see Picture 39.

No. 52 The Almshouses in Rookery Road, 1990

In the Middle Ages the villagers looked to the Lord of the Manor for almost everything in their lives — work, home, help and protection. As circumstances changed and the population grew this dependence on local landowners also changed, and by the time of Queen Elizabeth I there was a fair amount of poverty all over the land. Beggars and wanderers were a common sight. Eventually Poor Laws were passed by Parliament to try to do something about it and each parish became responsible for its own sick and poor people. Things stayed this way until the latter half of the nineteenth century.

The Almshouses in Rookery Road were built in 1716 and bear a date stone and inscription "The poor ye have alway". They were to be "for honeste poor persons to dwell therein" as long as they didn't "teach any schoole or sell ale, syder, perry, brandy or other liquors." They are now privately owned and were restored in the 1980's. The car space on the left was a village pound; the white building on the right now called "Delma" was a nail warehouse in the mid nineteenth century, and by the end was a butcher's home and shop.

John Holloway

No. 53 The Barracks, Common Road, late 1930's

People and places acquire nicknames in a variety of ways, but no one remembers why these houses became known as "The Barracks". They were built before 1800 and lasted over 150 years. Perhaps it was because two of them were tall with three storeys and such buildings were rare in Wombourne then. The little one with its chimney pressed up against its neighbour must have been squeezed in later, for building land was scarce in those days, as every available square inch was under the plough and owners were in no hurry to sell. There is no evidence of any soldiers billeted there, so I assume "The Barracks" was yet another friendly nick name which stuck.

The picture was either in 1935 for George V Jubilee or 1937 for George VI coronation. The residents did well with their decorations — they had some good ladders or someone did some acrobatics out of the bedroom windows, and proud to do it.

Modern houses, nos. 19 and 21, now occupy the site.

Dorothy Whick

No. 54 Harvest time in Common Road

Until the 1950's the present centre of Wombourne was "the village" with lanes connecting it to the hamlets of Blakeley ("the Common"), Bratch, Giggetty and Ounsdale. The land in between was arable and many men and women worked in agriculture or horticulture, either full time or seasonal. This typical country scene was taken where now stands house No. 40 looking towards Lower End. The building on the left was one of the village's three nail warehouses in the nineteenth century; next to it are "The Barracks" (see picture 53). The nailer's cottage on the right is the only survivor of a cluster of old dwellings here on Common Road — it was tastefully enlarged in the late 1980's. All the fields in this area were worked by the farmer from the Mill House (see picture 55).

Look at the face of young Roland Jones on the leading horse — if anyone was enjoying that long ago summer day, he was!

William Sadler

No. 55 The Mill House Farm, Common Road, 1901

When the farm land here was developed it was a pity that this fine house was not incorporated into the builder's plans, only the trees in the garden remain and have given their name to Pinewood Close. Close by was the site of an ancient water mill and its pool reached back — almost to Lower End Bridge. It was a corn mill at first but became a hammer mill during the civil wars in the seventeenth century for making armaments. By 1800 the name had been shortened to "The Ham Mill" and Ham Mill Meadow is the old name of the land, now Wombrook Walk, near the Lower End Bridge on Common Road side.

A footpath from Common Road crossed behind the house to the mill site and the brook. The owner tried to have it closed but the parish Council disagreed; it is perpetuated by a short path at the bottom of Glendale Drive.

Lloyd Sale Catalogue

No. 56 Wombourne Common/Blakeley, 1930

In a village where the name is spelt with the final 'e', and without it, and Billy Bunn's Lane can have one 'n' or two, everyone accepts one of its hamlets with two names — "Blakeley" answers to "Wombourne Common" and vice versa. Before the nineteenth century the eastern boundary of the common followed the line of Giggetty Lane beginning at Clap Gate House, to Sitch Lane and Green Hill Farm. The arable land on the village side was called "Blakeley Field" and when a hamlet grew up on what had been the common close by, both names were used to describe it, bringing confusion to the visitor but not the locals.

Wombourne "proper" was almost foreign parts a mile away across the fields, and the hamlet was a world on its own. A track out of Common Road was recorded as "Grassy Street" in the 1881 census, to the residents it was "up the Grass" — it was up-lifted to Park Avenue when extended in the 1930's. Most of the houses in the picture have been replaced, the entrance to Wombourne Park is now at near right.

Walker's Series

No. 57 The old Swan pub at Blakeley, c1960

Although Blakeley was little more than a handful of cottages it had a Wesleyan chapel, two pubs and two shops. This pub, the Swan, was replaced in the 1960's, the other, The Mason's Arms served its last pint about 1900, and after being a dwelling house for half a century, became a fish and chip shop.

The old Swan was a typical little pub, a bar and a snug with a connecting passage leading to a hatch which served as an off licence. My mother brewed our beer so I only saw the inside if I went with children going for their father's supply. The landlady's bottle-filling ritual for child customers fascinated me; she put a tun dish down the narrow neck filled the bottle to overflowing and put the cork in. Then came the intriguing bit — she moistened a label in the beer slops and stuck it over the cork and down both sides. It was years before I found out that she had to do this by law, so that it could be seen if it had been tampered with on the way home. I bet there were one or two youngsters who tried.

No. 58 The Bread Van, 1920's

Hughes's shop at Blakeley fulfilled most general needs — from cheese and sugar to bootlaces and cotton, from bacon to soap, buttons and lamp oil! Behind the shop was the bakery out of which every day, except Sunday, came the unforgettable smell of warm new loaves and cakes. Is it just pure nostalgia or was the bread really nicer then? Comparison can only be made in the memory, and memory is well known for playing tricks.

It was delivered while still warm to the cottages and here is Bill Piper with the day's load, including young Cliff Brooks whose father was Hughes's excellent baker. The horse knew the route as well as Bill did and could almost have done it on his own. I asked a 1990 milkman if he would like to return to the days of horse drawn floats and he answered emphatically "Yes. I would be able to call the horse on, and he'd catch me up, but I can't do that with me electric van!"

Marjorie Brooks

No. 59 A Wombourne Common Wedding, c1909

A wedding at Wombourne Common Methodist chapel joining together the Nock and Hughes families. The ladies in their best gowns and hats — what superb deportment they had in those days. Such clothes and headgear certainly called for a dignified walk, no room for slouchers then. But I'll guess that the men, smart as they were, couldn't wait to get out of those high starched collars.

The bride and groom surrounded by those they loved, and all in serious pose — they daren't move or even smile in case the picture was spoiled, but what a lovely picture they make.

The church was built in 1891 and has had several alterations through the next century, the last major project was in the early 1980's when the porch in the picture was removed so that a vestry could be built, and the interior plan reversed. The main door is now on the left side.

No. 60 The Blakeley Mission, Chapel Street, 1890-1957

The Rev. William Heale wrote this in the magazine, May 1890: "the long desired object of the Blakeley Mission room has now been realised. On April 19 the building, erected by Mr. Hiram Carrier, which though unpretentious is generally acknowledged to be pleasing in appearance as well as suitable for its various uses . . . was dedicated by the Ven. Melville Scott, archdeacon of Stafford . . . our thanks to all who have freely given the use of their homes for meetings, especially Mrs. H. Tranter who has opened her home twice a week for seven years, at which attendance was so large as to make this room a necessity." The cost was £200, mostly gained by house collections. It was replaced by the new church of the Venerable Bede in Giggetty Lane in 1957. The old building was sold and made into a private dwelling.

Chapel Street got its name from a Methodist meeting house lower down from the Mission, earlier in the nineteenth century.

No. 61 The day the King was crowned, 1901

The ladies had just finished their high tea on Edward VII's coronation day, the men had tucked into a beef dinner, the children had sports and tea. This segregation came to an end when they all trooped up Big Hall Hill at Withymore for the great bonfire and fireworks. They wandered home very late and exhausted . . . except for the young couples, well it was dark on the hill when the bonfire had died away . . .

Family albums everywhere have pictures like this, a bunch of good neighbours enjoying themselves. These ladies had more than a hundred children between them and no miracle gadgets to shorten their 36 hour days. My grandma Isabella — first right next to Kitty Cowern, I wish I knew all their names — had a few frills on her starched apron I notice, and what about all those smart straw boaters! When all was over, I doubt that Edward in all his glory had had a better day.

No. 62 Snow at Blakeley corner, April 4 1950!

Five shops and a post office occupy the corner where Common Road joins Giggetty Lane. They were built in 1957 on part of the garden of Blakeley House.

Previous to this development there were three large boulders by the hedge near the house gate, and they came in handy as seats for the oldest inhabitants when they were putting the world to rights. When I look at the picture above, it stirs a memory of a frosty New Year's Eve just after the war when a road night watchman had set up his brazier by the stones and I sat there with a little group of locals listening to the church bells. One of the men, an ex-soldier, had been a Wombourne ringer before the war, and he told us how he and another local man had been invited to join the German ringers in Cologne cathedral to ring a peal when peace was declared. In the light of the fire we watched him as he recalled that happy day and shared its joy again with us.

No. 63 The Cross Roads, Wombourne Common

Not a good picture, but it shows how the cross roads looked before the fields on each side were built over, now Wombourne Park. This is the point where the B4176 Bridgnorth Road crosses the one from Wombourne to Swindon. A footpath from Sitch Lane came out at the stile on the field corner, a pleasant place to sit and enjoy the view across Smestow and Black Hills.

In 1650 the Bridgnorth Road was part of the main coaching route from London to Holyhead through Meriden, Birmingham, Dudley, Bridgnorth, Much Wenlock, Shrewsbury and on through Wales. There is a map of it in Dudley Reference Library, one of many made by John Ogilby (1600-1676) who was famous for his strip maps of the coach roads. In the eighteenth century Thomas Telford cut a way through Tettenhall Rock thus improving the route through Wolverhampton — soon to be preferred by travellers — and no longer was the coachman's horn heard as the big horses raced over Wombourne Common down to the Smestow river and the road to Halfpenny Green.

Walker's Series

No. 64 Nailer's Row Giggetty Lane 1951

This was the last time harvest would be gathered in on Blakeley Field. Within six months of the picture being taken, a gap was made in the hedge and the builders of new houses moved in. Anciently the hedge was where part of Wombourne Common began, and when the Row was built it was on land which had recently been open heath and copse. The hamlet of Blakeley was growing up, mainly nailer's cottages and these six, built between 1820 and 1840 were the last word in worker's accommodation — one room down, nailshop joined on at the back, one bedroom and a tiny closet, pigsty and "midden" up the large garden.

When the nail trade finished in the late 1880's the back rooms became wash houses and later kitchens, and in the mid twentieth century had bathrooms built over the top. In the early 1980's they were saved from demolition, tastefully restored, and a wing added at each end making ten attractive dwellings, and thus enhancing rather than destroying the character of Nailer's Row.

No. 65 The Lido, 1932

Well, *we* called it "the Lido", even if it was only a deep hole in a sand quarry in Giggetty Lane. The day's workings in local pits were apt to fill with water quickly, and the sound of pumps running was a familiar sound at night time. This hole was a beauty, about fifteen yards wide, thirty long, and the pure spring water was fifteen feet at least at its deepest. In Wombourne in 1932 most children learned to swim in the canal or on the deep bends of the brook. A swimming pool of any sort was sheer luxury. I was not allowed in, that's me on the bank by a very young George Cowern, but it was a job to keep the men and boys out. The head belongs to Bill Horton, and as well there's Ken Massey, Archie Clark, my father, and one of the King boys (I think?).

The fame of the Lido reached beyond Wombourne and I can remember feeling quite peeved when "strangers" found our pool. Eventually someone found out how to drain it into the brook, (it was sand he was after, not water!) but we called him a few choice names for destroying our paradise.

After the land was reclaimed the Ambulance and Fire Stations were built on top, so, should they disappear one day, you'll know where they have gone!

No. 66 Longford, Giggetty Lane, c1920

"Longford" was on the Wombourne map before 1800 and it is the place where the Wom Brook crosses Giggetty Lane in the hollow a few yards north of Staffs and Worcs canal bridge "Giggetty" No. 44. A smaller stream, the Penn Brook now goes under the road a bit further on and joins the bigger one just below the footbridge. In earlier days when both of them were forded and untamed by tarmac and local councils, they joined where they wished, and thus in particularly wet times would make a long ford indeed!

In the 1930's the area was affectionately known as "Dickies Brook" after Richard Corns who farmed nearby and lived in Longford House up the road. You can see him on Picture No. 76, second from the right of the men sitting down. This is just one of several examples of a nickname taking over from the official one and becoming better known.

Walker's Series

No. 67 Longford—or as the children remember it—"Dickies Brook"

The view is towards Giggetty canal bridge — there are now houses on both sides and a high level footpath just over the bank on the right.

The picture was taken on a warm late May evening in 1957 and there was no harm in Rona, Cherry and Lesley paddling in the middle of the road, for cars were few and far between. To the left, where the brook runs under the canal, it was even deep enough for a few yards swimming. The broad bank was just right for picnics, drying off, or just idling away a couple of hours. At night it was a favourite with courting couples, but by the late twentieth century the increased traffic and buildings have put a damper on all these pleasurable activities. Nevertheless it is still a good place to ride through on a bike!

No. 68 Heath Mill 1974

The Smestow river, the Wom Brook and other fast tributaries of the River Stour, were harnessed from early times to power mills and forges. Heath Forge was in operation by the mid sixteenth century and was probably one of the sites used by Dud Dudley, an early pioneer in experiments smelting iron ore with coal instead of charcoal when it belonged to his father Lord Dudley. Later it was worked by the Foley family who became prosperous iron-masters and eventually bought the great house at Stoke Edith in Herefordshire in 1692. Because of that move the early documents pertaining to the Heath and other local forges are now held in Hereford County Record Office. They make fascinating study.

The Heath became a corn mill in 1827 when it was remodelled or rebuilt for Sir John Wrottesley, and was worked until the late 1930's. It was demolished in the 1970's for a large housing estate, and the developers were pleased to accept names with old associations for the new roads.

John Holloway

No. 69 The Pool at Heath Mills, 1930

The first pool built to supply the Heath Iron Forge in the sixteenth century was on the lower meadows near the works. In the late eighteenth century an upper pool was made near Ounsdale Road (as it was then) with water brought by a long leet from the Smestow in Trysull, and more from the Wombourne brooks. A workman's house by the pool soon changed the road name to "Pool House Road", and when the present large estate was built in this area in the 1970's the new roads were given names relevant to the iron trade and the masters, and the nature and former use of the surrounding countryside.

In my childhood it was deemed a local beauty spot, sadly lost when the pool was drained in the 1940's. Being shallow it froze quickly in winter and then all that was needed to turn the men (my father among them) into ice hockey stars was a smooth round pebble and stout sticks out of the hedge. Being only a little girl I was told to keep out of the way and "go slide near the edge."

Walker's Series

No. 70 The Waterfall, Heath Mills, 1930

This pretty waterfall was on the Wom Brook on the east side of the bridge over the Bridgnorth Road (B4176) at Heath Mill opposite the entrance to Smestow Lane. On quiet days the clear sweet water made music as it tumbled down; when it was angry and Guinness brown, the cream coloured spray rose higher than the banks, and when icicles dropped from the ledge it became a magic place, all "silver and glass".

It was destroyed when the land was being prepared for houses in the 1970's — "by accident" it was said. Such a shame! But it can live on, for those who remember, in this old picture.

Walker's Series

No. 71 The canal at Giggetty in its heyday

These buildings were a watch house and stable belonging to the canal company. The long garden was known as "The Pleck" an old Midland word for yard or garden. Two houses were built on it in 1989, and opposite, across the canal, is the Pool House Estate of the 1970's.

My great grandfather, Thomas Critchley, moved to this house from Stroud in 1855 to mine Wombourne's sand and then transport it to the industrial areas by narrow boat. Mother related how one of his horses had been a hunter belonging to "The Woodhouse", a particularly intelligent animal who needed few commands. He was an excellent worker and never put a foot wrong until his sharp ears picked up the distant sound of a huntsman's horn, long before the boatman behind him. He would atempt to gallop and the lurch he gave the boat would almost pull it out of the water. Old habits die hard, but apart from a few swear words, his antics caused more laughter than sorrow.

Walker's Series

No. 72 Looking north from Giggetty Bridge, 1920

On the right is a wharf and crane; next, two cottages which were already old when James Brindley's navvies dug away half of their gardens in 1766 for the new canal; Lindale Drive is now on the field beyond — its old field name was "Hungry Grey" because it was greedy for manure; and just below, on the bend, the canal was widened so that the boats could turn. There were seven wharfs between Wombourne Bridge (nicknamed the Brickbridge now) and Ounsdale, and at the time of the picture were all in use for sand, coal and timber.

The Round Oak pub at Ounsdale is just visible through a gap in the trees. Read what I have written under picture No. 76 and imagine the men on the way home from the pub sitting here contentedly in the bullrushes by the towpath, whiling away a summer afternoon. It was a pleasant place to sit anyway, and folks didn't seem to be in such a hurry to get to tomorrow, as many of them are today.

No. 73 The "Good Intent" at Giggetty Wharf, 1926

The "Staffs and Worcs" canal, opened in 1772, connects the Trent and Mersey canal at Great Haywood with the river Severn at Stourport, a vital link in the great plan of inland waterways connecting the Mersey, the Humber, the Thames and the Severn with the whole country.

From Wombourne went its good sand to the industrial acres of the Black Country and views like this one were familiar by the "cut". In this case it is the "Good Intent" being loaded just north of Giggetty Bridge with sand and gravel. She was registered at Wolverhampton as No. 1116 by F. & H. Critchley on April 20th, 1925 as a "dwelling" in which could live "in the after cabin, three adult male persons, or, three adult female persons, or, a man, his wife and two children under twelve."

I have often wondered why grandfather Fred chose that name for his new boat, what happened to it after he retired in 1933 (aged 83!), and of the people whose whole working life was centred on that little cabin, the boat and the canal?

No. 74 The hamlet of Ounsdale—up to the 1950's

Ounsdale, a mile west of the village centre on the Bobbington Road, grew up after James Brindley brought his lovely Staffordshire and Worcestershire canal down the Smestow valley on its way to Stourport in the late 1760's. Modern dwellings have replaced the old cottages, the left hand one of the row was an early pub called "The Navigation". Ounsdale School now occupies the field at top right; the Mount Pleasant is just visible top left, and the Round Oak is by the canal bridge — hard working navvies and boatmen got very thirsty!

Ounsdale is a corruption of "Holendene" the name of a village open field in the Middle Ages and thought to come from Old English words for "holly" and "valley". Various spellings came between that and the present Ounsdale — on Brindley's bridge No 45 it is "Houndel" because that is how the locals said it, and some still do.

Walker's Series

No. 75 The Round Oak, Ounsdale, 1950

The Round Oak pub is at the side of the canal at Ounsdale, and for most of the twentieth century was known as "Spark's" after two landlords, father and son, both named Jim Spark. Its description in 1808 was "warehouse and shop, house and stable" but by 1834 was officially the "Round Oak". The stables opened on to the towing path and a flight of stone steps led up to the front of the building. There were wharves on both sides of the canal. The door on the left led to the shop; the post box is in the wall.

This canalside pub still caters for boatmen, who though only now pleasure bent can still work up a thirst. By the time they reach Ounsdale they have either just negotiated the three locks at the Bratch and need a drink because of their efforts, or about to take them on — and therefore feel like a drink first!

No. 76 Outside the Round Oak at Ounsdale, c1914

The landlord James Spark the first (third from right), his wife and daughter, six customers, the postman, two dogs, three different kinds of hat and a jug of ale. Perfect company, strong beer and rich conversation; what more could a chap want?

My mother would smile when she recalled how some of the Oak customers got home when she was a child in the 1890's. They lived at the Giggetty so went along the towing path. If the weather was fine and the mood was right each would throw a matchstick into the water at "Houndel" Bridge and then bet on which would get to the next bridge first. How they knew them apart is a puzzle! The canal was busy then and every time a boat passed the matchsticks either got lost in the wash, or started going back towards Ounsdale, a circumstance which could lengthen the race by hours! It seems that neither the cross waiting wives or the ruined dinners spoiled the fun.

Weyman & Connie Jones

No. 77 The Mount Pleasant Public House, Ounsdale

It is hard to say whether this is a Victorian or Edwardian picture with only the clothes as evidence, but one thing is certain — it was a Banks's house then. In the mid twentieth century it was a Free house, at the end of it it is "M and B". When it was built there were no houses between Ounsdale and the top of Windmill Bank, just a long narrow lane.

The field opposite was anciently "Houndale Field" and a footpath went diagonally across it to Planks Lane ending near the present old railway bridge at a point called Middle Stile. It was probably closed by the farmer in the late nineteenth century although there are no official records of this happening. It was certainly a quick way to the village.

A post war road near to the pub has taken its name and is Mount Pleasant Avenue.

Donald Linney

No. 78 Wartime 1916 Ounsdale Road

No. 12589 Rifleman W. H. Crook, King's Royal Rifle Corps died of wounds received in France, aged 21 and was buried with full military honours in Wombourne churchyard on July 13, 1916. The picture was taken on the new Ounsdale Bridge of the still uncompleted railway line to Kingswinford. The Mount Pleasant pub at Ounsdale can be seen in the middle distance.

There are six boy scouts at the head of the procession and I assume they belonged to a local troop. I am sure this was a day they remembered always, the high black hearse, the plumed horses and the long slow walk to the church.

Dennis James Crook

No. 79 Wartime 1916, on Church Hill

The burial of No. 12589 Rifleman W. H. Crook, aged 21, July 13, 1916 (see Picture 81), and practically all Wombourne was there. It was the first military funeral of the 1914-18 war and the volleys fired across his grave were aweful and strange. There were three more local men to follow him —

Pte. E. J. Massey 22138, 6th Btn. King's Own Scottish Borderers, aged 19, of Giggetty, Oct 18, 1917.

Pte. L. Hale, 28082, 5th Btn. Grenadier Guards, aged 21, of Bratch Lane, Jan. 30, 1918.

Pte. J. W. Guest, 54471, 3rd Btn. Sherwood Foresters, aged 40 of Station Road, April 8, 1919.

— and the other 34 are still in France . . .

Dennis James Crook

No. 80 Planks Lane, 1945

Planks Lane runs from the village centre to Giggetty canal bridge. "Plank" or "Planke" is a Middle English word used to describe a piece of land longer than it was broad, usually about an acre. On the 1808 map of Wombourne there are eight of these divisions from Windmill Bank westward marked as "The Plankes", and the road name now has nothing to do with an old popular belief that it was because there were planks over the brook at the bottom before there was a proper bridge, in any case there were planks over all the brooks once! The name was in common use before the seventeenth century and the land was part of the big open Blakeley field which reached from Sitch Lane across to present Ounsdale Road.

In 1945 it was still narrow except for railway bridge approaches with grass in the middle where wheels didn't touch, wild flowers covering the high banks. And in the days when they rang the school bell, if you heard it at the bottom of the lane, it seemed like ten miles to School Road! The adjacent fields were built on in the 1960's. In the picture the gate is about the site of the present Dale pub.

A. Clark

No. 81 Bratch Station, Great Western Railway, c1927

"Once upon a time, Wombourne had a railway . . ." and it lasted less than fifty years. A line from Wolverhampton to Bridgnorth via Wombourne, with a branch to Kingswinford, was planned first in the late nineteenth century, but only the branch came to fruition. Work began in 1913, stopped during the First World War and the line was not ready for traffic until 1925. After running for passengers at a loss for seven years, it became "goods only" for the rest of its time — except on special occasions like the village annual school outing in the thirties, and for the reception of ambulance trains at Wombourne station during the second world war.

When it was all over in the 1960's, the District Council bought the land and made it into a pleasant railway walk, with an information centre in the old buildings at the Bratch.

P.S. (I recommend to you Ned Williams' book "The Railway to Wombourne" which contains a detailed history of the line.)

Walker's Series

No. 82 The Railway Line, 1954

A view northwards from Planks Lane to Ounsdale Road. Westfield School is under construction on the left. The field on the right was nicknamed "The Wilderness" in the twentieth century, until "Ounsdale Crescent" was built on it after the second war. In 1800 its name was "Bad Furlong", a common ancient field name for infertile ground, or land that needed manuring to get results. The recent nickname shows that modern farmers had trouble with it as well.

The "iron road" is no more, and this stretch is part of a long footpath called the Kingswinford Branch Railway Walk with the banks covered with trees and wild flowers. There is a path along the west side which gives easy and safe access to the schools on Ounsdale Road. People walk now where the railway ran, a fact which certainly didn't enter the minds of the fellows who sweated for so long building it.

A. Clark

No. 83 When they built the railway . . .

If you read Ned Williams' book about Wombourne's railway you learn what a long while it took to get it built. This picture shows the first slice out of the woods on the Bridgnorth Road in 1913, but the Great War got in the way and work ceased. In 1922 the parish council asked the G.W.R. Company to "complete the work, as it would be beneficial to the residents, market gardeners, farmers and allotment holders." The answer was in the negative "as at the moment they could not incur any capital expense." One councillor was so angry he wanted the District Council to oppose any other scheme the G.W.R. might come up with! In March 1924 the railway company wanted to extend the completion date to 1927, but the District Council *did* oppose that one, and it was promised for December 1924.

When the line was opened in May 1925, all Wombourne cheered, and the parish council named the lane to the Bratch "Station Road" in celebration.

Skelding, Kingswinford

No. 84 The Bratch Locks, 1990

If you rush all the time you only half live, and then need pills to slow you down. The world's quiet places are better than pills. Take the Bratch locks, for instance, and enjoy them on an August day when the sweet pink balsam is five feet high round the canal ponds and there's a soft wind blowing the scent across to Orton Hills. Watch the boats as they go through the locks; they can't rush even if they wanted to because the locks have set the speed, and all boatmen can do is respect it.

James Brindley's flight of three locks was one of the major engineering works on the canal. He began building at Compton in 1766 and worked down the valleys to the Severn and for the first five miles the land fall was only 30 feet. At the Bratch it fell 30 feet in as many yards, hence complications in construction and water supply, and later alterations. The octagonal toll house is a striking feature. Read Ian Langford's "Towpath guide to the Staffs and Worcs Canal" for a comprehensive account of the whole of this attractive waterway.

Ned Williams

No. 85 The Bratch Pumping Station 1897 or "Bilston Water Works"

The Vicar wrote in the church magazine in March 1890 that the parishioners were furious over "proposals by Bilston Town Commissioners to sink wells at the Bratch." At a public meeting in the schools on January 27 they had passed a resolution "that all proper steps be taken to resist and avert such an injury." All to no avail, and in 1893 construction began of a pumping station to supply Bilston with water.

The villagers moaned that their wells would go dry, and a good number did, so the parish council appealed to Bilston Commissioners as "since they had been pumping, many homes had been without clean water and alarm was spreading". Mains water was laid in 1897 and to appease the recipients, they were granted a 3½% reduction on their water rate until Wolverhampton took over the works in 1959. Cottagers with good wells used them 'til the 1930's.

The pumping station is a Grade II listed building of red brick with buff and blue decoration, with a handsome castellated engine house with corner turrets. The picture, taken a year before completion, was one of a series taken by Whitlock Bros.

Wolverhampton Public Libraries (Bilston Collection)

No. 86 Bull Meadow Cottages 1901

These cottages snuggled against the wood on the bend where Orton Lane meets Billy Bunns Lane, and just across from the ancient "Bull Meadows". In the twentieth century they were made into one dwelling and became the home of Arthur Jenks, a member of the family remembered by "Jenks Road" for many years of service to church, parish and district. The property was demolished in the 1970's and new houses occupy the site.

The ancient woods still make a lovely back-drop for the village and long may they continue to do so. Pickerells Hill on the right was mined for sand but nature has healed the scars.

Perhaps these cottages had something to do with Wombourne's mysterious "Billy Bunn" (about whom so many questions are asked) since they are at the end of "his" lane? Well, it's too late to ask them now!

Lloyd Sale Catalogue

No. 87 Ladywell Cottage 1901

Walkers on Orton Hills know the place where clear water drips from a fissure in the sandstone outcrop called "The Lady Well" — from "well, wella," old English for "spring". It is probably the one recorded as "The Woodwell" in the thirteenth century and later dedicated to the Virgin Mary when it was said to have medicinal properties. According to Hackwood in his "Sedgley Researches" (1898), the oblations at the Lady well were received by a hermit who shared them between the churches of Wombourne and Penn. He added "it is a favourite resort of persons of frugal minds, on pleasure bent, who ruralise in the adjoining wood, and then at the cottage partake of the cup that cheers."

The cottage was occupied until the 1930's, all that is left is a bit of the back wall and a heap of sandstone under the ferns and brambles. People have come and gone, but the water runs from the Lady well as sweet as ever.

Lloyd Sale Catalogue

No. 88 Orton Grange 1901

The adjacent manors of Wombourne and Orton were united on the marriage of Maud, Lady of Wombourne and Alan, son of Walter, Lord of Orton, sometime between 1200 and 1220. The name Orton, or Overton, is derived from Old English words "over" meaning "higher, upper," or "on the slope", and "ton" for "settlement".

The hamlet is pleasantly dominated to the east by Orton Hills, highest point, Bearnett Lane is 533 feet, (163 metres). There are several fine houses and this one, Orton Grange, is dated 1685. In 1901 it was described as a "superior yeoman's residence standing well back from the road with a fine view of Orton Hills from the front". There were then thirty acres attached to the house itself and the rent for land and property was £70 a year. It was sold in 1901 for £1500.

The land opposite is "Hope meadow" — hope comes from a word meaning "wet" or "marshy".

Lloyd Sale Catalogue

No. 89 All that's best in Britain

Wombourne's famous picture appeared in the Times on July 1, 1935: "High Summer, a cricket match in the Midlands . . . on village greens all over the country cricket was played in ideal conditions last Saturday. This picture shows the match at Wombourne in Staffordshire south of Wolverhampton, between the village team and Blakenhall, in a truly English setting."

It was the second XI, Don Henty and Harvey Trott were the bowlers and for me they have searched their brains to come up with the rest of the team. Their list is Frank Hall captain, and as well there was Edgar Elliot, Howard Rogers, Henry Bassano, Jack Davies, Bill Wardle and Bernard Rogers — they *think* that is right, but the other two escape them. No wonder, it was fifty five years ago! Little did they realise as they "played up and played the game" that they were making a bit of Wombourne history in this pleasant picture. During the war it appeared in several publications including a book called "Beautiful Britain", and later as the above advertisement in many magazines. The manor house has gone and the village changed much, but thankfully in its green heart, summer Saturday afternoons are still like the one above; when the busy world seems to ease up a bit and no matter what battle is going on near the wicket, the overall feeling is of peace.

The Times

No. 90 And so, back to church . . .

You can't miss it, its lovely grey spire beckons from whichever direction you approach.

In this 1950's picture there is a bit of the old central wall on the left, the little arbour tree is just visible on the right in its railings. The yews by the path have grown a bit since, and the population of God's acre has doubled. Winter storms have broken the roof crosses; the wooden gate has gone, and thankfully so has the stopper which was just right for tripping over.

A lot of water has rippled down the Wom Brook since our early English forefathers built the first little church here in the tenth century with local sandstone and oak from the forest all around. Their descendants have altered, added and enlarged as fancy and need took them.

Wombourne, in 1990, has five churches: St. Benedict Biscop, and the Church of the Venerable Bede, both Anglican churches, one Methodist and one United Reformed Church, and St. Bernadette's Roman Catholic Church. Other denominations meet in various buildings. Their message is unchanging and ageless, and there is a blessing here for you, young and old, friend and stranger, whatever your memories . . . or dreams.

Maurice Smith